Sing A Song Of Safety!

Music by Gerald Marks
Words by Irving Caesar

'Each little song is a song with a lesson,
And this is the kind of a lesson we mean:
Stop, look and listen,
When traffic lights glisten,
And only cross streets when the red turns to green.

'Don't talk to strangers and don't play with matches.
These new little songs know the right from the wrong.
So learn while you're singing,
And sing while you're learning,
And you will grow up to be healthy and strong!'

HARRY N. ABRAMS, INC.
PUBLISHERS, NEW YORK

ISBN 0—8109—3800—6

Copyright © 1989 by Amsco Publications
A Division of Music Sales Corporation, New York, N.Y.
All rights reserved. International copyright secured

Published in 1989 by Harry N. Abrams, Incorporated, New York
No part of the contents of this book may be reproduced without
the written permission of the publisher
A Times Mirror Company

Art direction and design by Mike Bell
Illustrated by Mike and Joyce MacDonald

Printed and bound in Japan

Johnny be careful...
Mary beware!

Introduction

Toot! Toot!

Look out!

An Automobile Has Two Big Eyes

Oohh...it's hot!

Hot And Cold Water

14

Don't do...tricks!

When You Ride A Bicycle

Oohh!

Be careful!

Pins And Needles, Needles And Pins

I've lost my way!

Remember Your Name And Address

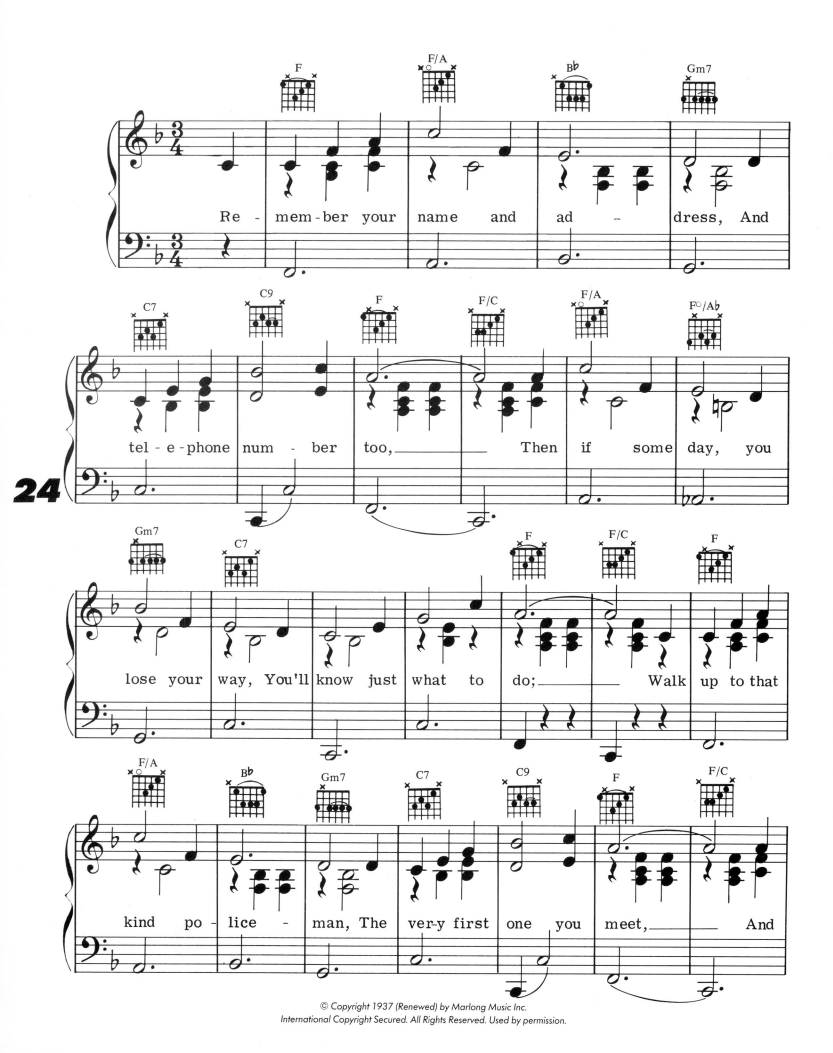

Don't lean out!

Leaning Out Of Windows

27

Help!

When You Swim

Don't strike the dog!

Striking Things

35

Stay Away From The Railroad Tracks

37

We're lost!

When You're Watching A Parade

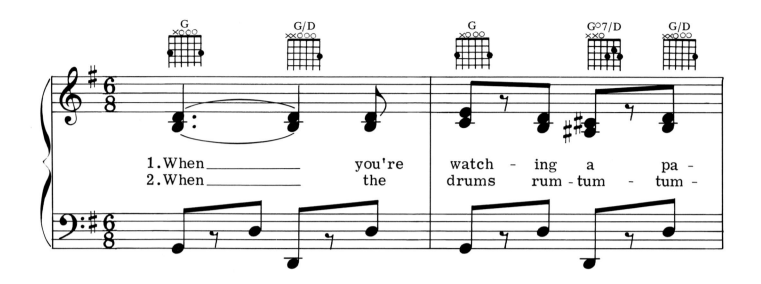

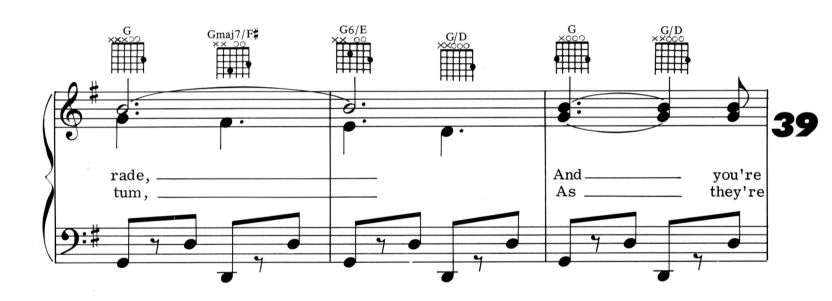

39

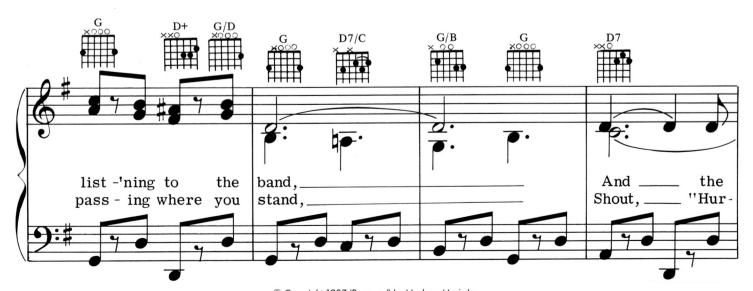

Look out!

Always Hold Your Umbrella High

With a bumpity bump!

Johnny Climbs Fences And Johnny Climbs Walls

1. John-ny climbs fen-ces, and John-ny climbs walls,
2. Just like a mon-key he climbs all a - round,

John-ny climbs ban-is-ters out in the halls. But
Then ver-y slow-ly re - turns to the ground. For

when he climbs fen-ces and when he climbs walls,
on-ly a mon-key can leap and can jump With-

John-ny is care-ful so he nev-er falls.
out com-ing down with a bump-i-ty bump.

47

Bang!

Pop-Guns And Rifles

Don't talk...

TO the driver!

Talking To The Driver

Thin ice will crack!

Ice Skating Is Nice Skating

57

Let the ball roll!

Let The Ball Roll

Don't throw stones!

Sticks And Stones And Bones

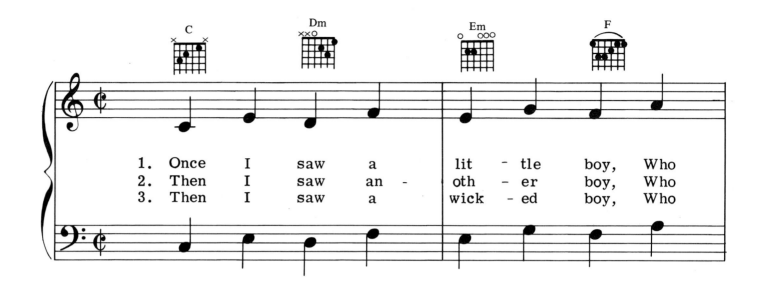

1. Once I saw a lit-tle boy, Who
2. Then I saw an-oth-er boy, Who
3. Then I saw a wick-ed boy, Who

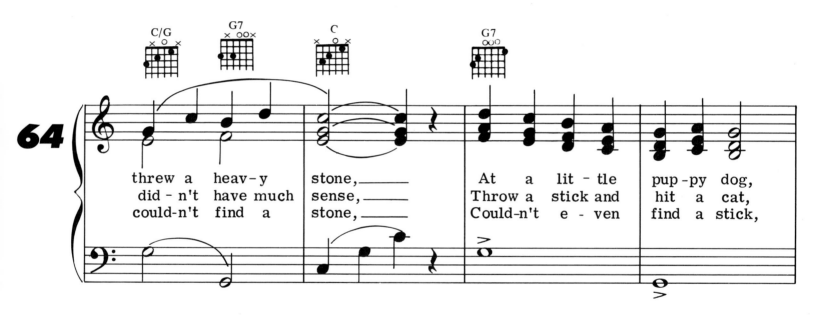

threw a heav-y stone,_____ At a lit-tle pup-py dog,
did-n't have much sense,_____ Throw a stick and hit a cat,
could-n't find a stone,_____ Could-n't e-ven find a stick,

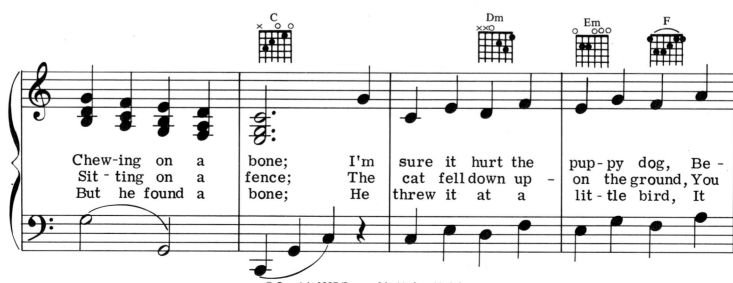

Chew-ing on a bone; I'm sure it hurt the pup-py dog, Be-
Sit-ting on a fence; The cat fell down up-on the ground, You
But he found a bone; He threw it at a lit-tle bird, It

65

I'm not afraid!

Never Be Afraid Of Anything

Don't play on the roof!

A Goof Plays On The Roof

Hip! Hip! Hurray!

Heroes Of Peace

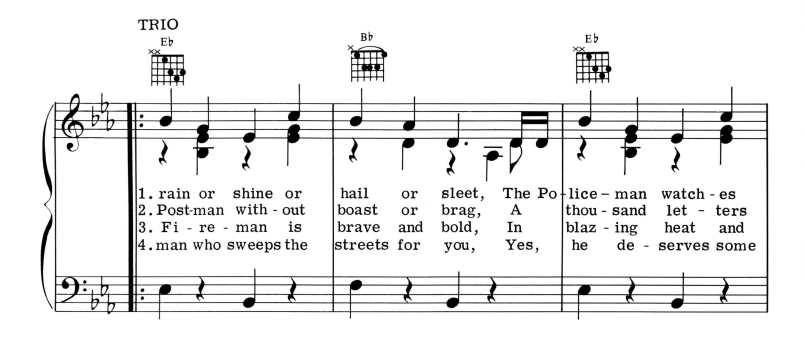

TRIO

1. rain or shine or hail or sleet, The Po-lice-man watch-es
2. Post-man with-out boast or brag, A thou-sand let-ters
3. Fi-re-man is brave and bold, In blaz-ing heat and
4. man who sweeps the streets for you, Yes, he de-serves some

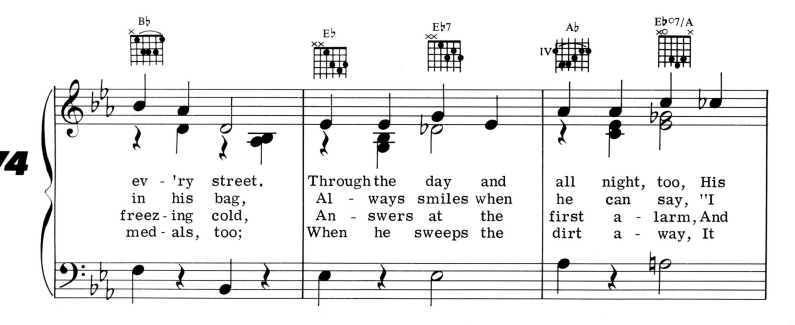

ev-'ry street. Through the day and all night, too, His
in his bag, Al-ways smiles when he can say, "I
freez-ing cold, An-swers at the first a-larm, And
med-als, too; When he sweeps the dirt a-way, It

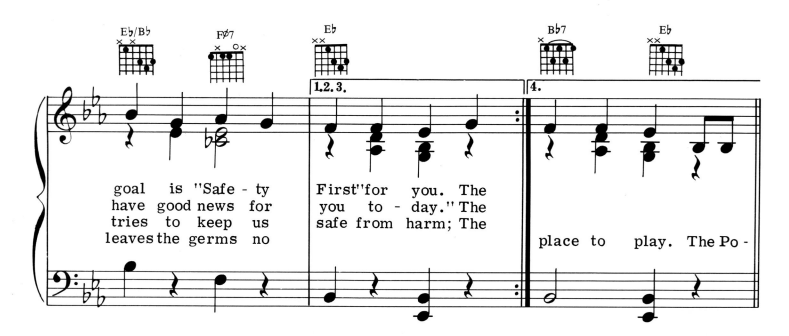

goal is "Safe-ty First"for you. The
have good news for you to-day." The
tries to keep us safe from harm; The
leaves the germs no

place to play. The Po-

We're All right...

We keep to the right!

Keep To The Right

ZZZZ